Fierce Fighters

GS

Charlotte Guillain

www.raintreepublishers.co.uk
Visit our website to find out more information about Raintree books.

To order:
☎ Phone 0845 6044371
▤ Fax +44 (0) 1865 312263
▣ Email myorders@raintreepublishers.co.uk

Customers from outside the UK please telephone +44 1865 312262

Raintree is an imprint of Capstone Global Library Limited, a company incorporated in England and Wales having its registered office at 7 Pilgrim Street, London, EC4V 6LB – Registered company number: 6695582

Edited by Rebecca Rissman, Nancy Dickmann, and Catherine Veitch
Designed by Joanna Hinton-Malivoire
Picture research by Tracy Cummins
Original illustrations © Capstone Global Library 2010
Original illustrations by Miracle Studios
Production by Victoria Fitzgerald
Originated by Capstone Global Library
Printed and bound in China by Leo Paper Products

ISBN 978 1 406 21610 3 (hardback)
14 13 12 11 10
10 9 8 7 6 5 4 3 2 1

ISBN 978 1 406 21714 8 (paperback)
15 14 13 12 11
10 9 8 7 6 5 4 3 2 1

British Library Cataloguing in Publication Data
Guillain, Charlotte.
Vikings. -- (Fierce fighters)
355.1'0948-dc22

Acknowledgements
We would like to thank the following for permission to reproduce photographs: akg-images pp. **8** (ullstein bild), **27**; Alamy pp. **14** (© North Wind Picture Archives), **19** (© Sherab), **21** (© The Art Gallery Collection), **25** (© Rolf Richardson), **26** (© Kari Niemeläinen); Art Resource, NY pp. **16** (© The Trustees of The British Museum); Corbis pp. **10**, **15** (© Werner Forman), **18** (© Bettmann); Getty Images p. **17** (Gary Ombler); Heinemann Raintree pp. **28 top** (Karon Dubke), **28 bottom** (Karon Dubke), **29 top** (Karon Dubke), **29 bottom** (Karon Dubke); Photolibrary p. **12** (CM Dixon); Shutterstock p. **9** (© ajt); The Granger Collection, New York p. **22**.

Front cover illustration of a Viking charge reproduced with permission of Miracle Studios.

The publishers would like to thank Jane Penrose for her assistance in the preparation of this book.

Every effort has been made to contact copyright holders of material reproduced in this book. Any omissions will be rectified in subsequent printings if notice is given to the publishers.

All the internet addresses (URLs) given in this book were valid at the time of going to press. However, due to the dynamic nature of the Internet, some addresses may have changed or ceased to exist since publication. While the author and publishers regret any inconvenience this may cause readers, no responsibility for any such changes can be accepted by either the author or the publishers.

Some words are shown in bold, **like this**. You can find out what they mean by looking in the glossary.

Contents

Raging raiders

Place: Village in north England
Date: AD 800

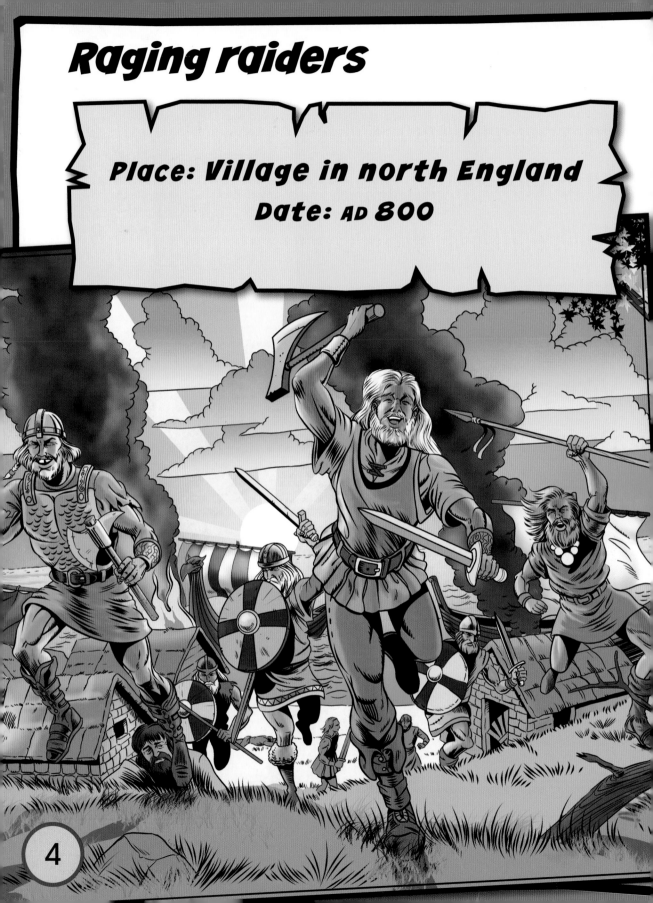

The village huts are burning. The villagers are dead or have run away. The fierce **warriors** are taking all the gold back to their ships.

The Vikings have **raided** again!

Viking timeline

800s AD	Vikings attack and rule half of England
1000s	Vikings settle in North America
1066	Vikings are defeated in England
1600s	People from Europe start to settle in North America
2000s	You are reading this book

Who were the Vikings?

The Vikings lived in Denmark, Norway, and Sweden. They spent most of their time farming and fishing. But they were also fierce **warriors**. They attacked and stole from villages and cities all over Europe.

Where the Vikings lived

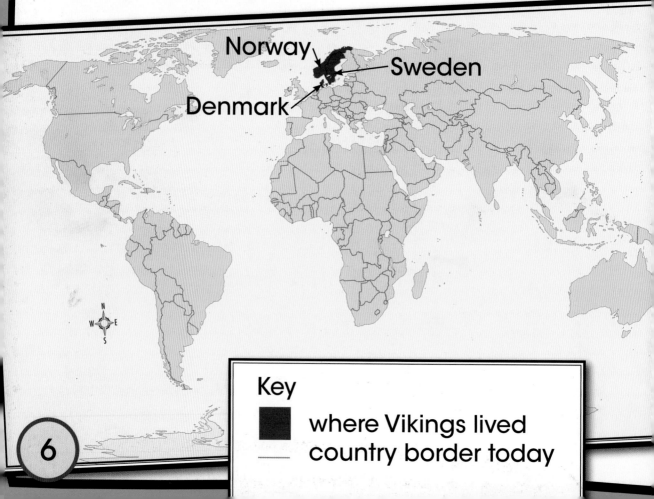

Norway

Sweden

Denmark

Key

where Vikings lived

country border today

DID YOU KNOW?

The word *vik* means "bay", and *ing* means "coming from". So the word Viking means "someone who comes from a bay".

Wild warriors

People all over Europe were afraid of Viking **warriors**. These fighters were very brave and skilled. They arrived quickly to **raid** a town. These attacks were a terrible surprise.

DID YOU KNOW?

Vikings raided other villages because they needed farmland.

Raiding Viking **warriors** killed anyone who got in their way. They took other people away with them to sell as **slaves**. They burned everything in their path and stole anything that was useful.

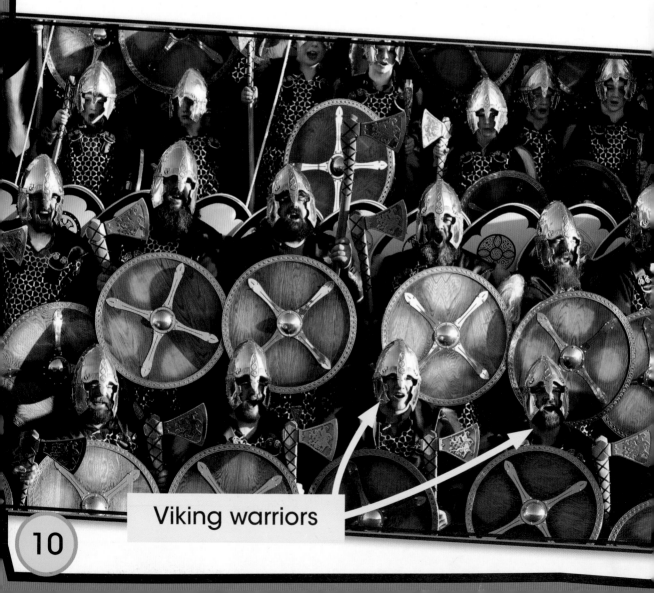

Viking warriors

DID YOU KNOW?
Vikings took cows, horses, food, and gold and silver on raids.

Berserkers

The fiercest Viking **warriors** were called **berserkers** (say *bur-zer-kers*). They were wild in battle. They bit their shields and ground their teeth. They didn't even wear **armour**!

DID YOU KNOW?
Some Viking stories tell of berserkers who fought naked!

berserker

These are pieces from a game.

Viking weapons

Viking **warriors** started battles with bows, arrows, and **spears**. When they got closer, Vikings would often attack their **victims** with their bare hands.

helmet

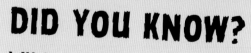

DID YOU KNOW?

Viking helmets were made of leather or iron. They never had horns or wings attached to them!

Swords were very important. Viking **warriors** often gave their swords names. They were buried with them when they died. They also used **battleaxes** and knives to fight.

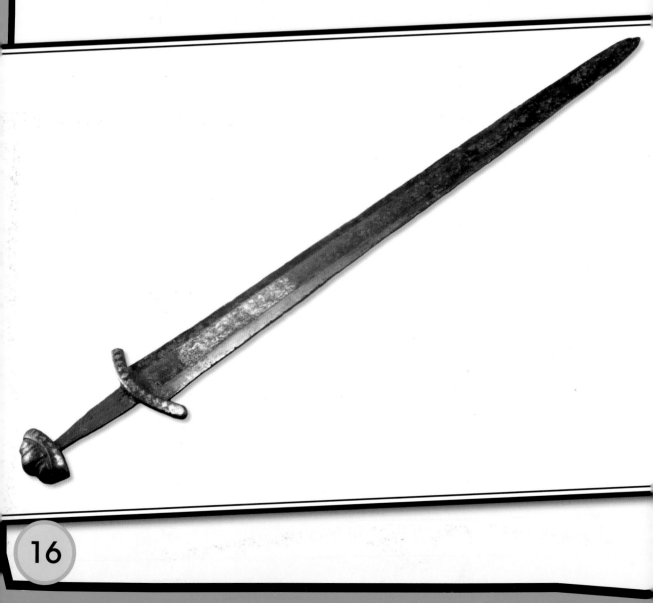

These axes were so sharp they could cut through a helmet and skull.

DID YOU KNOW?

Viking poems tell us about swords with names such as "war snake", "viper", and "battle-flasher".

Viking ships

Vikings used special ships when they went on **raids**. These **longships** could sail up rivers and land on beaches. Sometimes they had dragons carved on the front to scare their **victims**!

DID YOU KNOW?

Vikings took a bird called a **raven** with them when they sailed. If the Vikings got lost they let the raven go and followed it to land.

Death in battle

Viking **warriors** were not afraid of being killed in battle. They believed they would live again in a place called **Valhalla** (say *val-hal-ah*). They believed warriors in Valhalla fought all day and had parties all night. This was their idea of heaven!

DID YOU KNOW?

Viking warriors were buried with their weapons. They thought they would need the weapons to fight in Valhalla.

Famous warriors

Erik Bloodaxe was a king in Norway until his brother took over. Then Bloodaxe began **raiding** towns in Scotland and England. Stories about him tell of his huge **battleaxe** and his evil wife, Gunnhild (say *Goo-Neeld*).

This painting shows the warrior King Olaf leading a Viking raid.

Erik Bloodaxe

DID YOU KNOW?

Other scary Viking names were Thorfinn (say *Thore-fin*) Skullsplitter and Bjorn (say *Bee-yorn*) Ironside.

A Viking called Rollo led an army of **warriors** in France. The French king gave Rollo land to stop the attacks. Rollo took the land but carried on fighting!

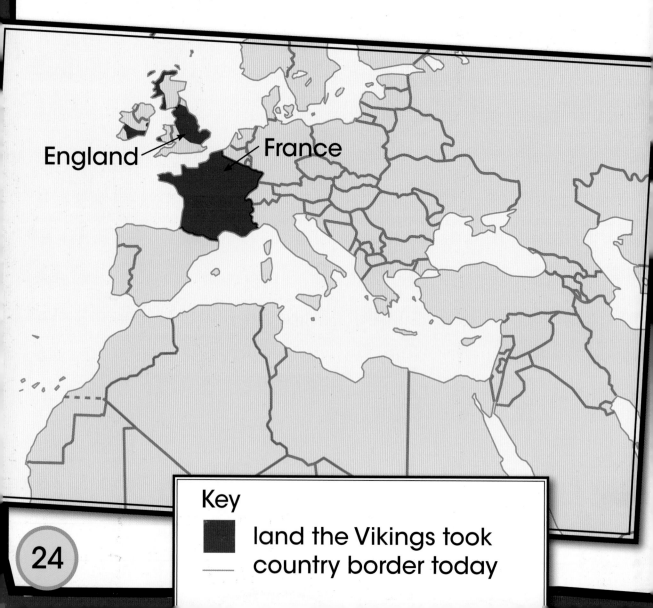

England

France

Key

land the Vikings took

— country border today

statue of Rollo

DID YOU KNOW?

Many Vikings stayed in northern France. They became the Normans and invaded England in 1066.

Viking women

Viking women looked after children, cooked, and made clothes. They did not go to war. But Vikings believed in flying **warrior** women called **Valkyries**. They thought Valkyries watched battles and decided who would die.

Valkyries

DID YOU KNOW?
Vikings believed Valkyries flew off to **Valhalla** with dead warriors.

Viking activity

Make a model Viking longship

You will need:

- pencil
- paints
- paint brush
- card
- a straw
- glue
- a small piece of modelling clay
- scissors

1. Fold a piece of card in half. Draw the outline of the side of a Viking ship, keeping the bottom of the ship on the fold.

2. Cut this shape out and stick the two ends together. Paint the boat brown.

3. Place a small piece of modelling clay in the bottom of the ship and stick the straw into this.

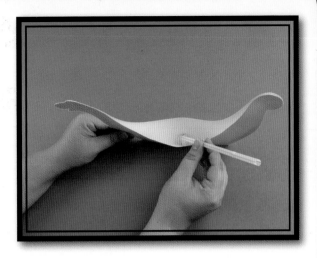

4. Draw a sail shape onto card, cut it out and paint.

5. Make two holes in the sail and push it onto the straw.

Your longship is ready to sail!

Glossary

armour covering made of metal or leather to protect a soldier

battleaxe large axe

berserker wild Viking warrior who did not wear armour

longship Viking boat that could sail up rivers and land on beaches

raid surprise attack

raven large black bird like a crow

slave person who is owned by someone else. Slaves had to work hard and didn't get paid.

spear weapon with sharp point on a long pole

Valhalla large hall where dead warriors fought battles and ate feasts

Valkyrie warrior women who watched Viking battles and took dead Vikings to Valhalla

victim person who is attacked or hurt

warrior fighter

Find out more

Books

Starting Point History:
Who Were the Vikings? J. Chisholm, S. Reid
(Usborne Books, 2002)

Vikings, Allison Lassieur (Capstone Edge Books, 2007)

Websites

www.bbc.co.uk/schools/vikings/
This website helps you to explore daily life for Vikings as
well as learn more about Viking raiders.

www.pbs.org/wgbh/nova/vikings/
On this website you can find out more about Viking
longships.

Places to visit

Jorvik Viking Centre, York

Travel back through time and visit a Viking town. You
can also see Viking helmets and weapons and a Viking
warrior skeleton!

The British Museum
www.britishmuseum.org/
You can find out more about the Vikings at the British
Museum.

Find out

What can you
find out about the
Viking god Odin?

Index